Artlist Collection
THE DOG
Happy Howliday Book

by The Do
As told to Howi

D1383250

Scholastic Inc.

New York Toronto London Auckland Sydney
Mexico City New Delhi Hong Kong Buenos Aires

ISBN-10: 0-545-03970-3
ISBN-13: 978-0-545-03970-3

© 2006 artlist INTERNATIONAL, INC.

12 11 10 9 8 7 6 5 4 3 2 1   7 8 9 10/0

Printed in China
First printing, May 2007
Designed by Angela Jun

It's a well-known fact: We Dogs love howlidays! Christmas, Hanukkah, Kwanzaa . . . no matter what the howliday, we say WOOF! Bring 'em on! And since we're not all Cocker Spaniels with roots here in the USA, a lot of us have wonderful and interesting traditions from other parts of the world.

Because no matter where you come from, chances are your howlidays include lots of food and family and plenty of human distractions. That means we Dogs can get away with loads of stuff. We can jump up on the bed, grab a drumstick or two off the counter, and sneak out the door. And with all that family around, we usually end up with a good belly rub no matter what!

Ahhhh, the howlidays . . . it's a fine time of year!

Now we're here to help you have the happiest of howlidays, too. We've put our favorite howliday songs, recipes, and activities in this book, plus some of our best howliday memories.

So throw a log on the fire, curl up under the tree, light a candle . . . and get ready to celebrate with the Dogs!

Howliday Sing-Along!

There's nothing like some classic carols to bring out the old howliday spirit. Here are the first few lines of some of our favorites to get you started!

HERE COMES PAPILLON
(to the tune of "Here Comes Santa Claus")
Here comes Papillon!
Here comes Papillon!
Right down Papillon's lane!
He's too small to have those reindeer —
That would be insane.
Fur that stands up, he's a cute pup
But far too small for might,
So don't expect a single gift
'Cause Papillon comes tonight!

JOLLY BERNESE MOUNTAIN DOG
(to the tune of "Jolly Old Saint Nicholas")
Jolly Bernese Mountain Dog,
Lean your head this way.
I know you just want to be
A friend in every way.
Howlidays are your best time
'Cause you like to please,
Wrapping gifts with your own paws
And scratching at some fleas. . . .

SANTA PAWS IS COMING TO TOWN
(to the tune of "Santa Claus Is Coming to Town")

You better watch out.
You better not growl.
Better not drool,
I'm tellin' you now.
Santa Paws is coming to town.

He's making a list,
Spendin' his days,
Gonna find out who sits and who stays.
Santa Paws is coming to town.

He sees you when you're digging.
He knows when you've escaped.
He knows if you ate all that steak,
So chew fast, for goodness' sake!

BRUNO THE LOCK-JAWED ROTTWEILER
(to the tune of "Rudolph the Red-Nosed Reindeer")

Bruno the Lock-Jawed Rottweiler
Had a very blocky head,
And if you ever saw it,
It could make you feel some dread.
All of the other puppies
used to hide beneath the bed.
They never played with Bruno
Until they knew that he'd been fed!

DECK THE DOG
(to the tune of "Deck the Halls")
Deck the dog with bones and ham hocks,
Fa la la la la la la la la.
'Tis the season all dogs eat lots,
Fa la la la la la la la la!

FROSTY THE BULLDOG
(to the tune of "Frosty the Snowman")
Frosty the Bulldog was a nasally challenged dog,
With two cropped-off ears and a smashed-in nose
And two eyes tucked in some folds. . . .

WE WISH YOU A HAIRY CARPET
(to the tune of "We Wish You a Merry Christmas")

We wish you a hairy carpet,
We wish you a hairy carpet,
We wish you a hairy carpet,
And a furry New Year!

Much shedding we bring
To you and your kin,
Much shedding and some barking
And a furry New Year!

WINTER WEIMARANER
(to the tune of "Walkin' in a Winter Wonderland")

My fur is gray, can you see me?
So are my eyes and ears and nose-y.
A beautiful sight
Against the snow white,
Walkin' with a winter Weimaraner.

Gone away is my long tail,
Here to stay is my docked tail,
But it can still wag,
though not like a flag,
Walkin' with a winter Weimaraner. . . .

UP ON THE GREAT DANE
(to the tune of "Up on the Housetop")

Up on the Great Dane,
Shih Tzus pause —
Such a large dog, such big claws —
How do we get down?
What have we done?
Why'd we climb the Great Dane?
It's not much fun!

Froehliche Weihnachten with the German Shepherd!

There's a legend in Germany, where I'm from, that says animals speak to one another on Christmas Eve. The legends also say the trees fill with fruit, mountains open up and are filled with gems, and church bells can be heard at the bottom of the ocean. I don't know if all of that is true, but I do talk to other animals on Christmas Eve (and the rest of the year, too).

I have lots and lots of howliday memories, because in Germany they start celebrating early — on December 6! On the night of December 6, the kids used to leave a shoe or boot for Saint Nicholas to fill with candy or twigs — depending on whether they'd been good or bad! (The hardest part for me was not chewing on the boot before they left it out.)

Of course, I also remember the beautiful Christmas trees that would appear on Christmas Eve. The idea of Christmas trees as we think of them now started in Germany, after all! It was like magic! There would be no tree. Suddenly, a bell would ring and we'd run into the front room, and there it was — a tree! It was usually covered with apples and candy and nuts and toys and tinsel and lights — all kinds of treasures. And there were plates of fruits and nuts, and chocolate, too! It was paradise. (Except for the chocolate, which is not good for dogs.)

So, except for the chocolate, Christmas Eve was all about eating.

What Dog wouldn't dig a howliday like that?

Paw-Made Gifts

You know the old saying "'Tis better to give than to receive"? Well, we believe that absolutely. That's why we're *giving* you a bunch of great ideas for presents you can make for US!

In fact, some gifts don't even need to be made. They just need to be found. The **stick**, for example. The finest gift a dog can get is a carefully selected stick.

Once you've found that stick, wrapping is a snap. A simple ribbon is the perfect accent for the well-chosen stick.

If you and your dog are already happy with your stick collection, consider **rope**! Of course, you can go to the store and purchase a "rope bone," but you can also make one.

Start with a thick cotton rope that's between one and two feet long. You don't want to use a rope that might cut your dog's gums, so make sure it's a soft rope. Decide which end is yours and which is for your dog. On your end, tie a simple knot so you can hold on when the tug-of-war begins. On your dog's end, tie a nonslipping loop so your dog has something to hold, too.

And, of course (need we even remind you?) a dog can never have too many **balls**. There's something to be said about any ball — tennis balls are fuzzy and fun, air balls are light and bouncy, rubber balls are good for nosing — you really can't go wrong. Just be sure you don't give your dog a ball that's *too small* because that could be a choking hazard.

•**NOTE:** The key to all these presents is that the only way we can use them is if you play with us!

We realize you might want to spend a little time on gifts for the rest of the family. We understand. It's not all about us. (It's just mostly about us.) Anyway, here are some suggestions for great presents you can make for anyone.

Knot-Edged Fleece Blanket

1. The most important part of making this gift is picking out just the right **two pieces of fleece**. Most fabric stores have lots of different patterns and colors of fleece, so you need to think about who the blanket is for and what kinds of colors and patterns that person (or dog) might like. You will need **one 5-foot square piece of fleece in each pattern.**

2. On a flat surface, lay the two pieces of fleece so that the front sides of each piece are facing out. Match up all the edges. If the edges don't match exactly, trim carefully with sewing scissors. Be sure to ask an adult for help!

3. Cut a 3-inch by 3-inch square out of each corner.

4. Now cut strips all along the four sides of your blanket. These strips will be tied in knots to attach the top and bottom layers of fleece. Your strips should be 3 inches long (matching the corner boxes) and about $\frac{1}{2}$ inch thick.

5. Start at a corner and tie a double knot, using one strip from the top piece of fleece and one from the bottom. (Be careful to match up the strips. You don't want to end up with a spare strip on one of the layers!)

That's it! Once you've tied all four sides, you will have a double-warm, extra-cozy, perfectly decorated blanket!

What do you know? This is great for us, too!

Picture These Presents!

There are lots of things you can do with a few good photographs. You can use pictures of you, your family . . . or, hey! How about your dog?!

Picture Storage Box

1. Take a cardboard box and cover it with a collage of photos from magazines, attached with a glue stick.

2. Glue your favorite photo to the top of the box, and add a label to personalize it! Your label might say "Mom's Pix" or "Fido's Photos."

Mom's Pix

Scrapbook Collage

1. Choose a favorite memory and pick out a large frame.

2. Collect photos and mementos that relate to your favorite memory.

3. Arrange everything *before* you start gluing!

4. Attach it all with a glue stick or fun stickers — be sure to fill the frame to the edges!

Button Frame

1. Dig up an old frame and any old buttons (or beads) you can find.

2. Attach the buttons and beads to the frame with white glue, and place your favorite photo inside. Instant gift!

A Shih Tzu New Year

A few of my relatives have memories of Christmas in China. My great-grandfather used to talk about the paper lanterns and trees of light covered in paper chains and flowers. He would tell me stories about waiting for *Dun Che Lao Ren* — Father Christmas — on Christmas Eve.

But what most of us with Chinese roots will always remember is the Chinese New Year! When I was a pup, I used to spend the day under the bed because firecrackers were going off everywhere! But once I figured out how much fun it is to dance around like a dragon to celebrate and honor all the Shih Tzus who have come before me, I couldn't wait for the celebration.

I have to be honest; there were a few other things that also helped me come to appreciate the howliday — food and gifts!

By the way, guess what 2006 is in Chinese tradition.

The Year of the Dog!

Feasting on Howliday Favorites

If you think it would be more fun to eat gingerbread in the shape of a cat instead of a little man, just use a kitty cookie cutter. That's what we do! Then woof it down!

Gingerbread is from Germany... just like me!

A Note from the Chef: If you have fur on your paws and forearms, you should probably wear plastic gloves. If you're human and mostly have skin, you can just wash your hands before beginning. And always make sure to ask an adult for help when you're cooking!

Gingerbread Cats

Ingredients:
$3\frac{1}{2}$ cups flour
1 teaspoon baking powder
1 teaspoon baking soda
1 cup brown sugar (packed tightly in the measuring cup)
2 teaspoons ginger
1 teaspoon cinnamon
1 teaspoon allspice
$\frac{1}{2}$ cup softened butter
$\frac{3}{4}$ cup molasses
1 slightly beaten egg

Instructions:

1. Mix the dry ingredients together in one bowl.

2. Mix the wet ingredients (butter, molasses, and egg) in a smaller mixing bowl.

3. Add the dry mix to the butter mix to make the dough. (It will be tough by the end, so you might have to use your bare paws!)

4. Refrigerate the dough for one hour.

5. Preheat the oven to 350° Fahrenheit. Lightly grease a cookie sheet. Spread a little bit of flour onto the counter or cutting board where you're going to roll out the cookie dough.

6. With a rolling pin, roll the dough out so it's about $\frac{1}{4}$ inch thick. Then cut cookies out of the dough, using cookie cutters. (You can make them any shape you want, but we prefer little short-haired felines!)

7. Place the cookies onto the baking sheet about 2 inches apart. Bake for 10 to 12 minutes.

8. Let cool, and decorate each cookie with frosting and candy.

Nothing reminds me more of the howlidays than a wee bit of Irish soda bread. It's easy to make, too!

A Note from the Chef: If you want to taste the batter, please use a spoon. Licking the bowl with your tongue is bad manners. If anyone sees you do it, you'll have a tough time getting them to taste what you've baked.

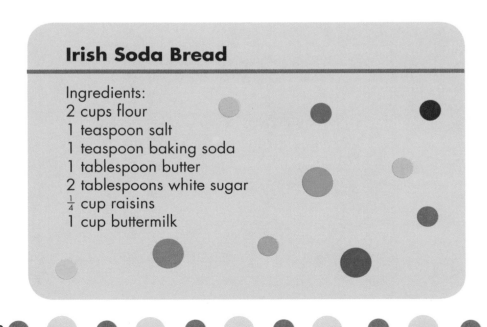

Irish Soda Bread

Ingredients:
2 cups flour
1 teaspoon salt
1 teaspoon baking soda
1 tablespoon butter
2 tablespoons white sugar
$\frac{1}{4}$ cup raisins
1 cup buttermilk

Instructions:

1. Mix the flour, salt, and baking soda together in a bowl.

2. Using your fingers, mix in the butter until the flour mix feels soft and crumbly.

3. Add the sugar and raisins, and mix well.

4. Mix in the buttermilk. (The dough should be damp and stretchy, but you should be able to pick it up.)

5. Preheat the oven to 350° Fahrenheit. Lightly flour a baking pan. Dust the countertop or a cutting board with flour and put the dough on it.

6. Knead the dough. (That means push your paws — or the heels of your hands — into the dough. Push it down into the counter, then forward. Then fold the dough in half and do it again.) Keep kneading until the dough feels well mixed.

7. Form the dough into an oval shape a few inches high. Dust it with flour and put it in the floured baking pan.

8. Use the backs of your paws (or hands) to flatten the dough down to about $1\frac{1}{2}$ inches high.

9. Bake for $\frac{1}{2}$ hour, or until it's golden brown. Let the bread cool for an hour before cutting.

What's Your Favorite Breed of Cookie?

Can you look at the cookie shapes on these two pages and tell which cutter would make which breed of cookie? Write your answers in the blanks below the pictures.

1. _____

2. _____

3. _____

4. _____

5. _____

6. _____

7. _____

Answers: 1. Greyhound; 2. Boxer; 3. Pug; 4. Bulldog;
5. Golden Retriever; 6. Chihuahua; 7. Basset Hound

A Scottish New Year to You!

Being a Shetland Sheepdog, I think fondly of old Scotland during the howlidays. Christmas is a rather quiet howliday back home, but I always think about Scotland at New Year's, or as we liked to call it —**Hogmanay**!

That word comes from a very tasty oatcake that all the children eat on New Year's Eve — unless, of course, they have a clever dog nearby who gets it first!

I remember one year, I was the first to set foot in our neighbor's house. They made such a fuss because of a tradition called "first footing." You see, folks in Scotland believe that the first to enter a home in the New Year affects what kind of luck the people who live in that home will have in the coming year. Strangers bring the best luck. Some believe a dark-haired stranger brings better luck than a fair-haired stranger.

Personally, I think a Shetland Sheepdog standing in your doorway at midnight on New Year's Eve is just about the luckiest thing in the world!

Finding That Howliday Spirit!

It doesn't matter where on earth you celebrate the howlidays — there's one thing everyone has in common. There are certain times of the year when everyone seems to think about helping others. Of course, there are ways to reach out to others all year long, but it seems like the howlidays really get folks thinking!

We Dogs try to be helpful all year long. . . .

Rescue Dog

Guide Dog

Search-and-Recovery Dog

Sled Dog

Here are two ways you can help others during the howlidays and continue helping during the rest of the year.

1. Adopt a Senior

Older people often find themselves alone at the howlidays. There are probably senior citizens right in your neighborhood who could use a new friend! The howlidays make it easy to break the ice — you can visit with a group of carolers, make a wreath and bring it by, or visit to help hang howliday decorations. Once you've made contact, keep that friendship alive through the rest of the year.

2. Recycle Gifts

Here's an idea that's good for people *and* the planet. Look around your room. How many toys, books, and clothes do you see that are in good shape, but are never used or are outgrown? Now think about all the stuff in the rest of your house, friends' houses, and your neighborhood. If you collect gently used items, clean them up a bit, and package them, you can be sure there are plenty of organizations happy to take the donation. You can start by calling local houses of worship, local shelters, the Salvation Army, or the American Red Cross.

Use these two pages to make some notes about the ways you're going to reach out to help others in the coming year. (And don't forget about the animals. They need your help, too!)

Who or what do you want to help?

_____

_____

How do you want to do it?

_____

_____

_____

_____

Who or what do you want to help?

_____

_____

How do you want to do it?

_____

_____

_____

_____

Who or what do you want to help?

_____

_____

How do you want to do it?

_____

_____

_____

_____

Who or what do you want to help?

_____

_____

How do you want to do it?

_____

_____

_____

_____

Who Gives to Whom?

Christmas is celebrated in a lot of different places, and the giver of gifts has a lot of different names! And since we Dogs are from places all over the world, we would know!

Here are some interesting howliday spirit names you can use to stump your friends and family.

ENGLAND
Father Christmas
(Bull Terrier, Beagle, Jack Russell Terrier,
Cavalier King Charles Spaniel, Border Collie)

FRANCE
Père Noel (Father Christmas)
(Papillon, French Bulldog, Bichon Frise)

GERMANY
Christkind
(A beautiful girl with a crown of candles)
(Poodle, German Shepherd, Schnauzer,
Dachshund, Rottweiler)

HOLLAND
Saint Nicholas
(Dutch Shepherd, Stabyhoun,
Kooiker Dog—Dutch Decoy Spaniel—,
Keeshond)

ITALY
La Befana
(A kind old witch)
(Italian Greyhound, Maltese, Spinone)

SPAIN AND SOUTH AMERICA
The Three Kings
(Ibizan Hound, Pyrenian Mastiff)

RUSSIA
Babushka
(A grandmother)
(Siberian Husky, Karelian Bear Dog,
Black Russian Terrier, Borzoi—
Russian Wolf Hound)

SCANDINAVIA
Different Christmas Gnomes
(For example, one is called Julenisse)
(Pomeranian, Norwegian Elkhound,
Icelandic Sheepdog, Swedish Vallhund)

Good Jul from Switzerland and the Bernese Mountain Dog!

Christmas back home in Switzerland is a lot like Christmas in the United States. I remember all the December days hectic with decorating and shopping and baking. *Yum!*

Christmas cookies are some of my happiest memories. I love eating *mailaenderli* (butter cookies), *zimstern* (cinnamon stars), and *spitzbuben* (jam cookies).

Of course, it was always fun to be in on the secret decorating of the tree so that the children could be surprised by Christkind on Christmas Eve. Santa Claus doesn't deliver the gifts in Switzerland. Christkind does — just like in Germany. And in some parts of Switzerland, that doesn't happen until January 1 or even January 6!

Howliday Word Search

Can you find the howliday words in the puzzle on the next page?
We've also thrown in a couple of dog breeds, too!

Advent
Boxer
Candles
Christmas
Claus
Collie
Corgi
Dreidel
Hanukkah
Kwanzaa
Mastiff
Menorah
Pointer
Santa
Shepherd
Spaniel
Stocking
Terrier
Tree
Unity
Wreath

```
D U C T F D V E I A X R N R N N A R R L L T C R P
O I N O S C R R L O C O M E A R P T I A E A O S N
A R C I L P P K L S D E L U N H E W A H S T L T T
B A L H T L S A S G E R I L E R R T R P R M N S R
Q E A E R Y I E U T H I R K R E D P L R K S S T R
P S A R M I V E O O F E N I A I R W P A N A D E B
K A H L H E S C A O I D E T L D T I E T N F A T F
E S N E S W S T U R D R H L H E S T E T N P E I I
T A T I P E A T M P E T O S T E L E A W M E Y T W
O A A L M H T H O A T S T N F T P W A A N H V I O
I M T R S E E R H C S L I S R P Z R I R F L D R
R M A C E R A R P X K N H T L O E E A S E D T A
L N E S O D E N D T E I N C A S U I E P H P K N E
H E H N T P I H Y I S G N U R A S N I C R U O G
R H R E O I A L E E E R S G S E V B A T A D S S C
G T S I L R F N D S A D S U L C S P D T E F H L L
U R N N E T A F A A R E N A T E I E H H E R R M E
C A T D A C T H T E C U E S A H E N L R R D U S S
E O E R O S A O I O T I E R A A L R A D R E A A A
A T R M S A Y D S L T I E K A Z I E T C N R I X R
V S T G Z S E S L S Y X K S O I S E I S L A T L H
R T H N I L A O C N O U T N H R N A C N B L C D R
I G A A A I R A E B N H U I R E X N N C A L T A I
T W A O N A A A I A P N S Y T S P I D P W P W I L
K C A N D S E S H U S N N K A U R A I F K T S E I
```

(Answers on Page 79)

Merry Christmas, but most of all, Happy New Year from the Akita!

Dried beans: *not* for dogs

The most important thing I can tell you about Christmas in Japan is that *Hoteiosho*, our Santa Claus, has eyes in the back of his head. That means he can *really* see you while you're sleeping — and doing everything else, too!

A lot of the Western Christmas traditions have been adopted in Japan, because Westerners are the ones who brought the idea of Christmas here! (Japanese people love to exchange gifts, so the idea caught on quickly.) You can be sure you'll have some turkey on Christmas Day in Japan, and probably see evergreens and mistletoe, too.

What I remember most, though, is the New Year! You've never seen a clean house until you've spent New Year's Eve in Japan. (It's tough to be a shedding dog at this time of year.) After the cleaning comes the decorating. Then all the people get dressed up and the father leads the family through the house to drive out evil spirits. (I like to bark at this point.) The father also throws dried beans in the corners of the house to push out the bad luck and welcome in the good. *(Dogs, do not eat these beans!)*

THE CANINE CALENDAR OF HOWLIDAYS

How to Celebrate Throughout the Year with Your Dog

New Year's Day
January 1
Ask your dog to make resolutions. Write them down.

_____

_____

Martin Luther King Day
Third Monday in January
Celebrate the equality of all people (and dogs).

Groundhog Day
February 2
Free your inner terrier and chase a small furry creature into a hole in the ground.

Valentine's Day
February 14
Hug your dog!

President's Day
Third Monday in February
Spend the day looking at pictures of pets that have lived in the White House.

Mardi Gras
The Day before Ash Wednesday
Make a mini parade-float for your pooch.

St. Patrick's Day
March 17
Let your dog eat green things.

April Fool's Day
April 1
Tell your brother or sister that your dog ran away. When he or she goes to look for him, get the ice cream out of the freezer and split it with your dog.

Easter
Let your dog help you hunt for hidden eggs.

Earth Day
April 22
Let your dog dig as much as possible, then plant something in the hole!

Mother's Day
Second Sunday in May
Get a puppy for your mom!

Memorial Day
Last Monday in May
Salute heroes — human and canine.

Flag Day
June 14
Help your dog design a flag for the United Federation of Dogs.

Father's Day
Third Sunday in June
Get another puppy, this time for your dad!

Midsummer Night's Eve
June 21
Stay up until midnight with your dog to celebrate the arrival of summer!

Fourth of July
July 4
Hold your dog's paw during the fireworks.

Friendship Day
First Sunday in August
Tell your dog that you are his/her best friend, too.

Coast Guard Day
August 4
Take your dog for a ride on a boat.

Labor Day
First Monday in September
March with your dog in the Labor Day parade.

Citizenship Day
September 17
Congratulate your dog for his/her leadership and commitment to making the neighborhood a cleaner, quieter place.

Columbus Day
Second Monday in October
Take your dog for a walk and discover a new land.

Halloween
October 31
Act frightened when your dog dresses up like a cat.

Election Day
Tuesday on or after November 2
Vote for your dog . . . no matter what.

Thanksgiving
Fourth Thursday in November
Set a place for your dog at the table.

Christmas, Hanukkah, or Kwanzaa
Include your dog in any activity that involves eating food or getting presents!

Don't forget that no matter what the howliday, your dog needs to stay safe and healthy. So keep in mind these howliday do's and don'ts!

Just Say YES!

Even though your howliday schedule can be hectic, don't forget that your dog needs **EXERCISE**.

A playful dog is a happy dog. So if you're in the gift-giving mood and wondering what to get your best friend, look for something that encourages **PLAY**. Think about a ball, a Frisbee, something to fetch, or something to chew — and you!

Don't forget to include your furry family members in as many activities as you can. Howlidays are great for families, after all — the *whole* family. Do your howliday **PHOTOS** include the dog?

Just Say NO!

POINSETTIAS are beautiful decorations for the house, but they can be poisonous to eat — so keep them away from us (and the cats, too).

Just because we like food, that doesn't mean we should eat *every* howliday treat in the house. Keep us on our regular diet — and definitely, **NO CHOCOLATE**!

Feliz Navidad! A Mexican Christmas with the Chihuahua

Every Chihuahua knows that *La Posadas* means Christmas.

The howliday begins every year on December 16, and lasts for nine days. Friends and families reenact the story of Mary and Joseph as they traveled from Nazareth to Bethlehem looking for a place to stay when the baby Jesus was born. Every night after dark, processions of family and friends playing their roles move from house to house. Each night, they are turned away from the houses. Finally, on the last night, Mary and Joseph are invited in and a great celebration begins!

And that means one thing — piñatas! Of course, as a Chihuahua I have always been too small to have any chance at breaking open the piñata. But being so close to the ground comes in handy once the piñata has been broken. . . . Candy and toys for everyone!

It's not hard to know when midnight arrives on Christmas Eve in Mexico, because fireworks explode everywhere. Bells ring and whistles blow, too. Many people attend church, and then everyone sits down to a big, traditional Mexican dinner.

By the time Christmas Day actually arrives, things are pretty quiet!

PICKING THE PAWFECT GIFT

It's not easy finding just the right thing for everyone on your list. What's good for the Poodle is not necessarily good for the Pug! We constantly have to think like another breed just to figure out what to get our friends for the holidays.

Write the gifts you plan to give to the people on this list.

Mom: _____

Dad: _____

Grandma(s): _____

Grandpa(s): _____

Brother(s): _____

Sister(s): _____

Aunt(s): _____

Uncle(s): _____

Cousin(s): _____

Friend(s): _____

Here are some fun gift ideas we came up with, breed by breed.

Pug
Goggles

Beagle
Nose plug

Pomeranian
Hairbrush

West Highland Terrier
Pogo stick

Cocker Spaniel
Earmuffs

Bulldog
Hankie

Chow Chow
Haircut

Shih Tzu
Headband

Corgi
Stilts

Dachshund
Hot dog bun!

Now comes the question of how to earn money to buy all those howliday gifts. Here are a few great, tried-and-true ways to make some extra cash:

German Shepherd
Security

Dalmatian
Fire Management

Siberian Husky
Transportation

Labrador Retriever
Wildlife Control

What can you do to save up some spending money?

1. _____

2. _____

3. _____

4. _____

5. _____

6. _____

A Visit from the *Jolasveinarnir* (the Yuletide Lads) with the Pomeranian!

When you come from a place that goes dark — both day and night — for a good part of the winter, and snow stretches as far as you can see, and the northern lights dance across the sky —well, it's not hard to believe that a man dressed in red can fly across the sky, pulled by reindeer.

In fact, I used to see reindeer all the time back home in Iceland. I never saw the flying reindeer, but they're very good for getting around on the ground, too!

But the real fun started on the twelfth of December. That's when the *Jolasveinarnir* — the Yuletide Lads — would visit all the good little boys and girls (and small fluffy dogs) and leave small gifts for them. Of course, you had to remember to put your shoes (or booties) on the windowsill at night.

For the twelve nights leading up to Christmas, we would get little gifts. Then, the Jolasveinarnir would return to the mountains. According to the stories, that is where they spent the rest of the year.

Doggy Chic for the Howlidays

In all the craziness leading up to the howlidays, don't forget to decorate the dog! We'd like to suggest some of the following ideas:

- A collar with mistletoe so that all smaller dogs (and cats) must be kissed

- Change fur color to red

- Change fur color to green

- Wrap tail in tinsel

- Ear ribbons

- Ornaments

- Lights

- Gift wrapping

Of course, we're *kidding*! Please DO NOT do any of those things to us for real! However, you are welcome to have a good time on the next few pages decorating our photographs! Don't forget the stickers!

Don't try this at home!

POODLE

SCHNAUZER

DALMATIAN

MALTESE

PAPILLON

BULLDOG

COCKER SPANIEL

DACHSHUND

Way Back When in Dalmatia (Yugoslavia) with the Dalmatian

It's true, I've spent a lot of great howlidays at the firehouse, but if I think way, way back, I can remember staying up all night on Christmas Eve with the humans to make sure the fire logs didn't go out. That would have been *very* bad luck.

I can also remember the children hoping they would get the gold coin that had been baked into the *Chestnitsa* — the Christmas cake. That was how it was back in Yugoslavia (in the region of Dalmatia) — the person who got the piece of cake with the coin in it would have good luck all year long.

But the most fun we had was on the two Sundays before Christmas. First we'd celebrate Mother's Day by playing tricks on our moms. We'd trap her in a chair until she gave us presents so we'd let her go. Then, the next Sunday, we'd do the same thing to our dads on Father's Day!

Sit! Stay! Waiting for the Big Day

Sometimes waiting for the big howliday to finally arrive can take forever! Here are a few ways to pass the time.
(We already gave you some of our favorite song lyrics, but here is a doozy of a song that might actually take a day to sing! So work on memorizing this song. The howlidays will be here before you know it!)

The Twelve Dogs of Christmas

For the first dog of Christmas, my trainer gave to me:
a Shih Tzu in need of a bath.

For the second dog of Christmas, my trainer gave to me:
two howling Hounds and a Shih Tzu in need of a bath.

For the third dog of Christmas, my trainer gave to me:
three wheezing Pugs, two howling Hounds, and a Shih Tzu in need of
a bath.

For the fourth dog of Christmas, my trainer gave to me:
four quite short Corgis, three wheezing Pugs, two howling Hounds, and
a Shih Tzu in need of a bath.

For the fifth dog of Christmas, my trainer gave to me:
five snorting Bulldogs, four quite short Corgis, three wheezing Pugs, two
howling Hounds, and a Shih Tzu in need of a bath.

For the sixth dog of Christmas, my trainer gave to me:
six Dachshunds digging, five snorting Bulldogs, four quite short Corgis,
three wheezing Pugs, two howling Hounds, and a Shih Tzu in need of
a bath.

For the seventh dog of Christmas, my trainer gave to me:
seven Pointers pointing, six Dachshunds digging, five snorting Bulldogs,
four quite short Corgis, three wheezing Pugs, two howling Hounds,
and a Shih Tzu in need of a bath.

For the eighth dog of Christmas, my trainer gave to me:
eight Shar-Peis wrinkling, seven Pointers pointing, six Dachshunds
digging, five snorting Bulldogs, four quite short Corgis, three wheezing
Pugs, two howling Hounds, and a Shih Tzu in need of a bath.

For the ninth dog of Christmas, my trainer gave to me:
nine Spaniels spinning, eight Shar-Peis wrinkling, seven Pointers
pointing, six Dachshunds digging, five snorting Bulldogs, four quite
short Corgis, three wheezing Pugs, two howling Hounds, and a Shih
Tzu in need of a bath.

For the tenth dog of Christmas, my trainer gave to me:
ten Terriers tugging, nine Spaniels spinning, eight Shar-Peis
wrinkling, seven Pointers pointing, six Dachshunds digging, five
snorting Bulldogs, four quite short Corgis, three wheezing Pugs, two
howling Hounds, and a Shih Tzu in need of a bath.

For the eleventh dog of Christmas, my trainer gave to me:
eleven Labs a-leaping, ten Terriers tugging, nine Spaniels spinning,
eight Shar-Peis wrinkling, seven Pointers pointing, six Dachshunds
digging, five snorting Bulldogs, four quite short Corgis, three wheezing
Pugs, two howling Hounds, and a Shih Tzu in need of a bath.

For the twelfth dog of Christmas, my trainer gave to me:
twelve Beagles barking, *eleven* Labs a-leaping, *ten* Terriers tugging,
nine Spaniels spinning, *eight* Shar-Peis wrinkling, *seven* Pointers
pointing, *six* Dachshunds digging, *five* snorting Bulldogs, *four* quite
short Corgis, *three* wheezing Pugs, *two* howling Hounds, and a Shih
Tzu in need of a bath.

Tasty Trivia for the Season

The traditional Ukranian Christmas meal is twelve courses! The youngest child in the family watches for the evening star to appear because then the feast can begin!

> I wish I may, I wish I might, have a place at the table tonight!

A long time ago in England, the traditional Christmas dinner was the head of a pig — prepared with mustard!

> Uhhh . . . maybe I'll just wait for dessert.

According to a survey, seven out of ten British dogs get Christmas gifts from their owners.

> What about the other three?!

The boxes for animal crackers — the Barnum's circus design — were made with a string so they could be hung on a Christmas tree.

Please hang them on a low branch for me!

Candy canes started as straight white sticks of sugar candy. A choirmaster at Cologne Cathedral had them bent to look like a shepherd's crook and gave them to children to keep them quiet during services. They became red striped in the 1900s.

From white to red striped? I don't think so!

An average of 1.76 billion candy canes are made during the holiday season!

Christmas! *Malanka!* New Year's with the Husky!

Here's how much we like Saint Nicholas in Russia: Many Eastern Orthodox Churches have been named after him, and Nicholas is one of the most popular names for Russian boys—even today!

So you can be sure we celebrate. In fact, there's Christmas, which happens on December 25, Ukranian Christmas on January 7, and *Malanka* on January 13!

I remember getting really hungry on Christmas Eve because all my people fasted that day, until after the church service on Christmas Eve. Then, what they ate after that didn't have any meat in it! But they didn't seem to mind. In fact, they seemed to be having a party. They were all eating out of the same bowl — something called *kutya*. That's a porridge made with wheat berries, honey, and poppy seeds, and it symbolizes hope, immortality, happiness, success, and untroubled rest. Personally, I'd rather have meat.

Some of my friends' families saved their celebrations for January 7. In the old days, some celebrated on Saint Nicholas Day. But no matter when it happens, children get gifts and people celebrate.

As for Malanka, now that's a party! We used to get dressed up and go to big banquets and balls. Malanka is all about being merry . . . as in Merry Malanka!

WHOSE HOWLIDAY DIARY IS WHOSE?

Read these Christmas and New Year's Eve Dog Diary excerpts. Can you tell which dog wrote which entry? (Here's a hint: Check out the howliday memories in this book. Pay attention to the different national traditions.)

Choose the dog sticker that matches up with the diary entry and put it in the box above the excerpt.

Dear Diary,
We started celebrating on December 6! It's just been nonstop since then. I'm so glad it's finally Christmas Eve, because I've eaten so much I don't think I'll be able to stand up for a week! This is not good. I'm a police dog, after all. I have work to do . . . *burp.*

Sticker

Dear Diary,
Please wake me up when it's all over. I can't believe they forgot to feed me and then just went out . . . for hours! Then, when they finally did come back home, what did they offer me? Porridge! Porridge? That's right. Porridge! And it didn't even have any meat in it. I can't tell you how ready I am for the New Year!

Sticker

Dear Diary,
I'm so glad Christmas Eve is finally here! It seems like ever since that day with the big turkey and the parade about a month ago, nobody has been home but me. My whole family has shopped and shopped and shopped. But the tree looks pretty with all those presents underneath it. I hear some guy in red is coming by tonight to bring more. But for tonight, we're all together, the stockings are hung, and tomorrow's dinner is already being prepared! (I hope dogs are invited.)

Dear Diary,
I must not eat beans. I must not eat beans. This is the hardest day of the year. Everybody is cleaning and rushing around, and I'm not supposed to shed or drool or bother anyone. Then, like that's not hard enough, they start throwing beans — ACTUAL FOOD! — into all the corners of the house and I'm supposed to just sit here! I will be good. I will be good!

Sticker

Mi amigo,
Ay, caramba! It's been a rough nine days. Every night I've
been getting dressed up in peasant clothes, which, let me
tell you, is not so easy when you're only a couple of inches
tall. But anyway, we've been going from house to house
looking for a place to stay. I'm happy to say that, tonight,
we were finally let in. All we've done since then is eat!
AY! What's that?! The sky is exploding!!

Dear Diary,
Please remind me next year that Christmas is only the beginning of the celebration. I completely forgot that the really big party happens a whole month later for our New Year. How could I forget about dancing around like a dragon? I am so exhausted that after all this I'm afraid I might sleep through the whole year. That would be very bad, because it's the Year of the Dog!

YOUR HAPPIEST HOWLIDAY MEMORY

_____

_____

_____

_____

_____

_____

_____

_____

_____

_____

_____

_____

_____

Answers from Page 37:

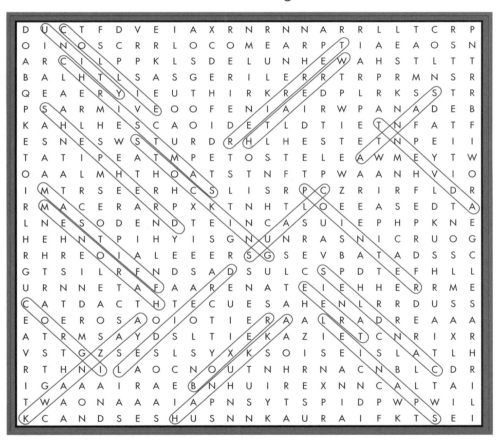

HAPPY HOWLIDAYS!